Media Literacy for Kids

Learning About Plagiarism

by Nikki Bruno Clapper

Consultant: JoAnne DeLurey Reed
Librarian and Teacher

raintree
a Capstone company — publishers for children

Raintree is an imprint of Capstone Global Library Limited, a company incorporated in England and Wales having its registered office at 7 Pilgrim Street, London, EC4V 6LB – Registered company number: 6695582

www.raintree.co.uk
myorders@raintree.co.uk

Edited by Gillia Olson
Designed by Cynthia Della-Rovere
Media research by Wanda Winch
Production by Laura Manthe

Photo Credits
All images by Capstone Studio: Karon Dubke except: Shutterstock: Multiart, cover (left), racom, 9

ISBN 978-1-4747-0430-4

Printed in China

Contents

What is plagiarism?

Plagiarism means using someone else's words, pictures or ideas as if they were yours. Plagiarism is a form of stealing.

People often learn by copying each other. It can be fun. But plagiarism is a bad type of copying.

Imagine that you write
a poem. Your friend enters
your poem in a competition
and says it is his. He wins a
prize. How do you feel?

Give and take credit

Your friend plagiarized. He did not give you credit for your work. When you write a poem, you own it. You are the author.

All authors deserve credit.
Giving credit is a sign
of respect. You say:
"This person had a great idea.
I want to share it."

Use sources the right way

An author's work is called
a source. Sources can be such
things as poems, drawings,
websites or videos. Sources
help you to write research reports.

You must always cite your sources, or give credit to the authors. If you do not cite your sources, you are plagiarizing.

When you use a source, describe the author's ideas in your own words. If you use his or her exact words, put them in quotation marks (" ").

Great ideas are everywhere.

Some of them are yours!

Now you know how to share

ideas without plagiarizing.

Activity: A story in your words

Practise using your own words by doing this fun activity.

1. Read a story that you like.

2. On a piece of paper, rewrite the story in your own words. Do not change the meaning of the story. Just retell it using different words. Now you have two versions of the story.

3. Next, ask a friend to read the story too. Do not show your version of the story to your friend. Then give your friend a blank piece of paper and a pencil. Ask your friend to rewrite the story in his or her own words. Now you have three versions of the story.

4. Swap pieces of paper with your friend. Read each other's version of the story.

What you need

2 pieces of paper

2 pencils

1 friend

5. Talk about these questions with your friend:

What was it like to rewrite the story? Was it easy? Was it hard?

Which retelling is most like the original story?

Which retelling is least like the original story?

Who is the author of the story? Why?

Glossary

author person who creates a work of art

cite give proper credit for the work of another person

credit recognition of an author

describe tell about something in words

deserve be worthy of something because you earned it

plagiarism copying someone else's work and passing it off as your own

plagiarize copy someone else's work and pass it off as your own

research studies about a subject

respect belief in the quality and worth of something or someone

source someone or something that provides information

version telling of something from a certain point of view

Read more

Get Writing! (Dream It, Do It), Charlotte Guillain (Raintree, 2014)

I Can Write Reports (I Can Write), Anita Ganeri (Raintree, 2013)

Websites

www.bbc.co.uk/bitesize/ks1/literacy/

Fun facts and activities to help you improve your writing skills!

23

Comprehension questions

1. Give some examples of sources.

2. Describe a time when someone copied you but it was not plagiarism.

Index